ASTROLOGY FOR CATS

by Simone Reyes and Ken Compton

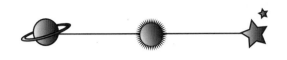

Cover Illustration by Design Dynamics
Typography by MarketForce

Published by Great Quotations Publishing Co.,
Glendale Heights, IL

Library of Congress Catalog Card Number: 97-77656

ISBN 1-56245-340-8

Printed in Hong Kong

Dedicated to our parents (Terry, Robert, Boyd and Mary) for teaching us to love animals and our four legged "kids" (Wanu, Diablo, Stevie and the late Lil' Feller) for allowing us to put their teachings into practice. And, of course, to all the animals behind cages, we are working to break the chain.

Simone Reyes

Ken Compton

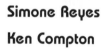

Introduction

For centuries we have known that the planets affect the earth and all of its inhabitants. The Zodiac holds the key to understanding, caring for and communicating with our family, children, spouses, co-workers, friends and yes.... companion animals! It is a given that cats mirror humans on basically every level. Cats have the unique ability to be loving, jealous, angry, guilty, shameful, playful, heroic and mournful. Just as the sign that we are born under governs our personality and affects our destiny, our beloved felines are born under stars that affect their (nine) lives as well.

4

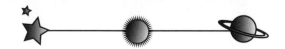

We have no doubt that the knowledge and insights you gain in this book, coupled with the Bach Flower Remedies we have included, will enrich the life of your cat beyond your beloved feline's wildest dreams!

* You will notice that we have used the words "he" and "she" interchangeably, except where we are referring to male and female cats in particular.

Quotation:

"Beware of people who dislike cats."

- **Irish proverb**

The Zodiac and Your Cat

How the Zodiac Can Bridge the Gap Between You and Your Cat

This book will help you understand the basic, inherent personality of your cat and will guide you through the school of feline companionship. It is our goal to incorporate the science of Astrology to offer answers to the most commonly asked cat related questions. It is our heartfelt belief that aquainting yourself with your cats visceral motivations will provide you with the tools you need to solve the majority of behavioral problems associated with your cat's sign and ultimately lead to a more harmonious coexistence between you and your companion animal.

It will help you determine if your cat is inherently people friendly, has difficulty relating to other cats, likely to be tolerant of babies and toddlers, likely to listen or ignore you, more inclined towards being a lap cat or an aloof loner & give you other important insights into your cats psyche. It will offer advice on such matters as if your cat will benefit more from the security of being in your home curled up in your bed or will he require a cat leash and long walks in the park. Is your cat a "toughie tomcat" or a gentle flower?

Knowing your cat's Sun Sign will give you answers to these answers and so much more!

7

Guessing Your Cat's Sun Sign

While it is impossible to know the birth dates of every companion animal, it is possible, with the help of our Feline-Sign test, to target the Sun Sign your kitty was born under. Once you attune yourself to your cats true personality, you will be able to answer this questionnaire with ease!

8

Sun Signs and their Meanings

A cat's Sun Sign begins to make its influence felt around the age of ten weeks, when a cat begins to move from kitten-hood into adult-hood. It is during this time that cats mature from their nursing, ultra mommy-cat dependency mode into realizing that he is his own cat and can make decisions on his own (i.e. using the litter box, eating solid food, going exploring, etc.). By four months, your cat's Sun Sign will be in full effect. Once you have found your companion cat's Sun Sign you will have a better understanding of the qualities that they possess, thus enabling you to be a more knowledgeable cat guardian.

9

Section 1: Guessing Your Cat's Element

Check off the groups of adjectives that best describe your cat. Limit your choice to one grouping. This will determine if he or she is a Fire, Earth, Air or Water sign:

-Fire: Outgoing, Fearless, Energetic
(ball of energy)

-Earth: Ego-oriented, Calm, Serene
(good old fashioned lap cat)

-Air: Vocal, Observant, Standoffish
(meow, meow, MEOW!)

-Water: Moody, Sensitive, Insecure
(melancholy baby)

10

Section 2: Targeting Your Cat's Personality

1. Decide which statement could best be spoken by your cat:

• "I'm the type of cat who could best be described as an interior designer kind of cat - I like to redecorate your furniture by putting my own brand of cat scratches on it. Try and try as you may to stop me, but I will not compromise my artistic creativity for anyone. I'm a real stubborn kitty!"

0 points

• "I'm the sort of feline who has her own agenda. I like to observe more than join in and can often be found with my tail in the air pretending not to hear you when you call my name. What can I say, if you want a companion animal who comes when you call, get a dog, darling!"

1 point

• "I'm the kind of kitty who loves to confuse you. One moment I am head-butting you, trying to get attention and the next I am running from your touch. I am a feline chameleon!"

2 points

12

2. Choose which celebrity your cat most closely mirrors in mannerisms:

Driven Madonna or Heavyweight Champion Mike Tyson

0 points

Ever-persevering Cher or "Comeback Kid" John Travolta

1 point

Chameleon Merryl Streep or Multi-talented Tom Hanks

2 points

3. Decide which personality portrait your cat falls under:

Personality #1: Aggressive, Instigating, Playful

0 points

Personality #2: Persistent, Relentless, Bull-headed

10 points

Personality #3: Whimsical, Fickle, Volatile

20 points

4. **Which type of music does your cat respond most favorably?**

Rap or Hard Rock – anything with a driving beat

0 points

Country or Easy Listening – music with emotion

1 point

Classical, Pop or Elevator music – anything goes!

2 points

5. What is your cat's favorite game?

Tug-of-War

0 points

Fetch

1 point

Stealing your socks

2 points

Part 3: EVALUATION

Add up your score to determine if your cat is a Type A personality, a Type B personality or a Type C personality:

1-10 Points: **Type A**

10-20 Points: **Type B**

20-30 Points: **Type C**

Now that you have determined which personality type your cat is, go back to Part 1 of this questionnaire and match your cat's element to the chart below:

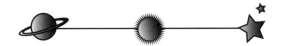

Fire + Type A	= ARIES
Fire + Type B	= LEO
Fire + Type C	= SAGITTARIUS
Earth + Type A	= CAPRICORN
Earth + Type B	= TAURUS
Earth + Type C	= VIRGO
Air + Type A	= LIBRA
Air + Type B	= AQUARIUS
Air + Type C	= GEMINI
Water + Type A	= CANCER
Water + Type B	= SCORPIO
Water + Type C	= PISCES

Congratulations, you have now determined your cats Sun Sign!

Chapter Three: Bach Flower Remedies For Your Cat

What are Bach Flower Remedies?

Dr. Edward Bach was a homeopathic doctor who recognized the unique power flowers could have over the human psyche and psychical body. During his years of practice in England in the late 1800s, he developed thirty-eight flower-based remedies to treat emotions, moods and mental tendencies.

It was his opinion that illnesses were always preceded by mood changes and a doctor who was able to recognize these changes could ultimately begin treatment of the disease before the actual onset occurred, lessening or halting the affect of the disease. Dr. Bach developed thirty-eight flower based remedies to aid in the treatment of his patients. Taken orally, they can significantly improve the emotional state of your kitty.

Cats, like humans, can benefit greatly from his remedies both physically and emotionally. Since they are natural, gentle and perfectly harmless, even a novice practitioner need not worry about administering the wrong dosage or remedy.

Why Should I Use Bach Flower Remedies on My Cat?

Just as the Zodiac affects a cat's emotional state, so does his environment. Similar to humans, cats sometimes need an extra boost from nature to help them deal with trauma. A trauma for a cat could include moving, separation from his mother, having a new cat or dog introduced into the family, mourning a family member who has passed away, etc. These remedies can also assist your cat to work out the emotional problems that he must face in his day to day life.

What is the Connection Between Bach Flower Remedies and the Zodiac?

The authors of this book feel that while any cat, regardless of his Astrological Sign, can benefit from these remedies, certain Sun Signs do especially well using specific Bach flower Remedies in particular. The first concern should always be targeting the emotional trauma the cat is trying to deal with and administering the appropriate remedy— so feel free to pick and choose. However, in this book of Astrology we have made specific mention of the unique Bach flower Remedy we believe will best serve the cat's Sun Sign.

How to Prepare and Administer Bach Flower Remedies:

Choose the Bach Flower Remedy or remedies you require by using the general suggestions that accompany your cat's Sun Sign or by scanning the entire list, Sun Sign by Sun Sign, for the specific problem your cat is having.

Then, into a one-ounce dropper bottle put two drops of each. Fill the bottle to three-quarters full with spring water. Shake vigorously 108 times. You may store this for fourteen days in your refrigerator.

23

Aries

21 March-20 April
THE RAM

Element: Fire

Ruler: Mars

Dominant Feline Aries Traits:
Adventure, Ambition, Assertion

Profile of an Aries Cat:

The Aries cat is full of boundless energy. This cat often greets you like a college frat buddy (usually after having just "decorated" your apartment with rolls of shredded toilet paper). Not to worry, Aries cats are much more than trouble! They are incredibly loving creatures who do not often engage in the popular feline sport of aloofness. In fact, Aries cats take no shame in tickling your toes with kitty licks to tell you it is time to wake up ALREADY. How is <u>that</u> for a good morning!

Aries pussycats will amaze you with their sweet disposition, even in times of desperation. An Aries cat may be feeling uneasy by the sight of a cat carrier parked by the door, but will rub up against your leg and trustingly allow you to put her in the box without so much as a hiss because she knows you only have her best interest at heart.

Purrs: The assertive nature of an Aries cat requires that her guardian be gentle, compassionate and, most of all, fun loving. An Aries feline will delight in playing cat and mouse with you-you taking on the role of the mouse of course! Try calling to your cat and then hiding behind a doorway, peek out from behind the door at your cat and then scurry away. Just watch your Aries cat hunt for you as she purrs so loudly your neighbors can hear her a mile away!

An Aries cat loves the sound of your voice. When you are talking on the phone, you will probably notice that your Aries cat dances around you in a state of ecstasy.

Why, you may ask? Because she is absolutely certain you are having a long, involved conversation with her!

28

Grrs: If left to fend for herself in the wild, this feline would take the position of either the leader of the pride or respectfully assign herself second in charge to a Leo cat. Therefore, you must never treat this kitty as anything but an equal member of your family. You must never raise your voice or speak down to your Aries pal, or she will disappear under your couch never to be heard from again.

Bach Flower Remedies for Aries Cats #1:

Agrimony: For the Aries cat who has difficulty being away from her pride. Aids in pulling her out of her shell, especially on days when she seems out of sorts. This remedy will give her a sense of security while she is at the vet or during times you are forced to leave your home for extended periods of time.

Bach Flower Remedy #2:

Chicory: For those Aries kitties who can be very possessive of their family. Especially useful for cats who use their claws as their primary means of communication. Encourages your Aries cat to show love in human terms—so get ready for lots of licking, Eskimo nose kisses and head-butting!

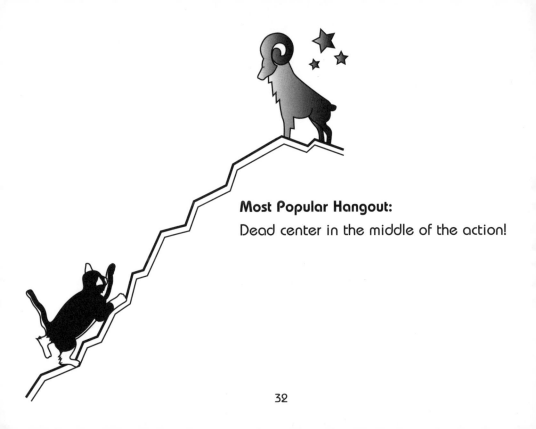

Most Popular Hangout:

Dead center in the middle of the action!

Favorite Cat Game:

Other than playing cat and mouse with you,
your Aries cat will take great pleasure in the fine
art of "zooming". That is, he will fly around your
house like a hurricane—occasionally knocking over any
breakables in his way. Dont fret—these zooming sessions
only occur about once a week, which should give you
ample time to clean up the mess before the next storm.

33

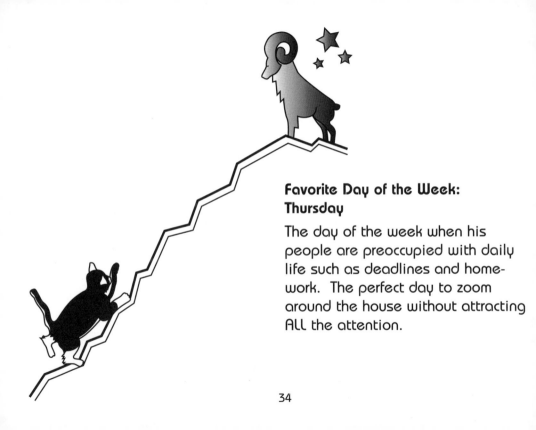

Favorite Day of the Week: Thursday

The day of the week when his people are preoccupied with daily life such as deadlines and home-work. The perfect day to zoom around the house without attracting ALL the attention.

Favorite Quote:

"The cat has too much spirit to have no heart"

- Earnest Menaul

Taurus

21 April-21 May

THE BULL

Element:
Earth

Ruler:
Venus

Dominant Feline Taurus Traits:

Stubbornness, Intelligence, Reliability

Profile of a Taurus Cat:

Cats born under the Taurus Sun Sign tend to be calm and predictable in their behavior-no real surprises here. Being around a Taurus cat will significantly lower your blood pressure, cure you of migraine headaches and will add years onto your life can't beat those statistics!

Taurus cats are the perfect companions for Senior citizens and the ideal partner for people afflicted with illness or bouts of depression. Their serene state of being radiates peace and contentment. Often referred to as the "angel cat" of the Zodiac.

Purrs: Taurus cats love to curl up in your lap while you read a book and wouldn't mind if you read aloud to him on occasion, too! They melt into their guardian's touch and yearn for their person to snuggle with them under the covers at bedtime.

40

Grrs: Taurus cats like each day to be refreshingly the same. They flourish in an atmosphere that is familiar and built on routine. While they enjoy the company of humans, they do not enjoy living with swinging singles or party animals. An occasional visit from a friend or neighbor is welcome, but they much prefer the relaxed familiarity of quiet family life.

Bach Flower Remedies For Taurus Cats #1:

Aspen: Great remedy for days when your Taurus pussycat must deal with dreaded changes in her routine. Quiets troubling fears and anxieties which suddenly appear without warning or reason. Gives courage.

Bach Flower Remedies #2:

Cherry Plum: Helps Taurus cats trust in their spontaneous spirit. Gives them the ability to explore the world and follow their heart.

43

Most Popular Hangout:

Under the bedcovers with just her tail sticking out.

Favorite Cat Game:

Practical Taurus cats enjoy the small things in life. Nothing makes her happier than the feel of digging her claws into a scratching post (she prefers the kind made of twine opposed to those of the carpet variety). She views her scratching post as an utter luxury, and does not take it for granted for even a moment.

Favorite Day of the Week: Monday

Her sensible nature tells her that Mondays are exciting because they signal the beginning of a new week where anything can happen.

46

Favorite Quote:

"With the qualities of cleanliness, affection, patience, dignity and courage that cats have, how many of us, I ask you, would be capable of becoming cats?"

- Fernand Mery

47

Gemini

22 May-21 June

THE TWINS

Element:
Air

Ruler:
Mercury

Dominant Gemini Feline Traits:
Alertness, Intelligence, People Friendly

Profile of a Gemini Cat:

Gemini cats are born explorers. If there is a way out of your house, a Gemini cat will find it (so please be sure to have an identification tag on her collar at all times!). They never really outgrow kitten-hood. The Gemini kitty can be friends with dogs and will adore the companionship of other felines.

They are natural show stoppers who may just surprise you by sitting at your window meowing at the moon just for a reaction. They often have a translucent quality to their coat and take great pride in grooming their fur. Their eyes glow so bright at night that they can illuminate an entire city street!

Purrs: Gemini's need to be free will put her at odds with domesticity. Therefore, you will need to entertain her by using a creative tool such as a flashlight. Try flashing the light on the ground in a zigzag motion and watch in amazement as your Gemini leaps, somersaults and attacks the light in a frenzy. She will be so grateful for having such a cool Mom or Dad to play with that you may have to set aside an hour each day for this special activity!

Grrs: Gemini cats hate to be restrained. So basic tasks such as clipping her claws may result in a showdown between you and your little companion. Never fear, her intelligent nature will allow you (eventually) to cut her nails as long as you supplement the experience with catnip, treats and loving praise from you.

Bach Flower Remedies for Gemini Cats #1:

Elm: Gemini cats often feel as if they can hardly contain their own energy. This remedy will help settle them down and restore composure when they can't seem to shake their desire to run around the neighborhood like a tornado.

Bach Flower Remedy #2:

Oak: Super remedy for spells when your Gemini starts to climb the curtains in your house out of boredom. The explorer in him makes him prone to periods of restlessness. Oak will give him the state of calm he needs to take a break from his cat world and wind down.

Most Popular Hangout:

In your backyard where she can often be found trying to dig a hole to China.

Favorite Cat Game:

Easily bored, this Gemini pussycat will seek out things to entertain himself and will not rely solely on his human to buy him tons of toys. He can often be seen gazing at the television, contentedly watching the nature channel.

Favorite Day of the Week: Wednesday

This Gemini Twin likes the feeling of being in the middle of the week because he can reflect on the past few days while planning cat excursions for the remaining days.

Favorite Quote:

"There is no snooze button on a cat
who wants breakfast."

- Unknown

59

Cancer

22 June to 22 July

THE CRAB

Element:
Water

Ruler:
Moon

Dominant Feline Cancer Traits:
Sensitivity, Moodiness,
Maternal/Paternal Instincts

61

Profile of a Cancer Cat:

Cancer cats are natural mothers and fathers who are instinctively gentle with children and the elderly. They are extremely sensitive and respond to gentle stroking and lots of good old fashioned T.L.C.

62

Their moods often fluctuate between behaving like loners to acting like one of the gang. Similar to the elephant kingdom, Cancer cats have very good memories and if treated badly, will not easily forgive the perpetrator. Their home is their island, and they are very protective of their surroundings. Be sure to have strangers approach with caution.

Purrs: This feline kitty needs to pampered like a baby. He loves to be carried in his guardian's arms with his ear cocked to you chest to hear your heartbeat (it reminds him of kitten-hood in the womb). You mus be an equal opportunity cat lover who doe not mind your feline friend climbing onto your dinner table during meals or onto the side of the bathtub to watch you shower.

Grrs: Don't attempt to roughhouse with your Cancer or you will find yourself being hissed-at or worse (a light hearted claw swipe isn't beyond the realm of possibility!). He does not appreciate having his tail pulled, his fur yanked at, etc. However, Cancer will tolerate this behavior from toddlers as they understand that little people can't seem to help themselves.

Bach Flower Remedies For Cancer Cats #1:

Hornbeam: Helps your Cancer cat get through the day when a mood has got her down. Teaches mental alertness and enthusiasm for life.

Bach Flower Remedies #2:

Red Chestnut: Cancer cats worry about their human family very much and often internalize these fears (which can lead to future medical problems). This special remedy teaches her the ability to think positive thoughts, let go of worry and relax.

Most Popular Hangout:

In the laundry basket or in the clothes dryer (so please check for your Cancer pal before you turn on your machine!)

68

Favorite Cat Game:

In Cancer's heart of hearts he yearns to play with other felines but this shy kitty will never be the first to initiate the first contact. To boldly approach another cat would horrify him since he likes to know what he is in for before he is smack in the middle of it. Therefore, do not push the issue when other cats are near. Instead, sit back and allow the other cat to approach first. You will see that in no time at all they will be stalking each other and having a grand ol' time!

69

Favorite Day of the Week: Tuesday

Families and single cat guardians often are home on Tuesday evenings as it is not a big date night. Therefore, this kitty can be sure to see his favorite people on this day.

70

Favorite Quote:

"People who hate cats will come back as mice in their next life"

- Faith Resnick

71

Leo

24 July-23 August

THE LION

Element:
Fire

Ruler:
Sun

Dominant Feline Leo Traits:
Pride, Confidence, Affection

Profile of a Leo Cat:

Felines born under the Leo Sun Sign love people, their abode and...trips to the groomer! Leo cats are born entertainers who will sprawl themselves across your finest piece of furniture, waiting for you to take their picture. They have been known to sit perfectly still for hours while an artist sketches their image!

They will charm company, even going so far as to unabashedly wrap themselves around a favorite person's leg before leaping into their arms without warning. Her cat eyes will pierce through you, flooring you with their power. They are jealous by nature so please always be mindful of his fragile Leo feelings.

Purrs: Cat brushes, combs, elixirs, collars with bows, bells, etc. are all the rage with Leo cats. They fancy beds lined with luscious fabrics such as velvet to sleep in. Praise this kitty 'til the cows come home and your feline will be eternally grateful.

Grrs: Leo cats do not like to be in a household full of other animals. They will tolerate perhaps one other cat for companionship but in no way will they tolerate rambunctious puppies or a bunch of other kitties running around vying for your attention. They are much too jealous for that crazy scene!

Bach Flower Remedies for Leo Cats #1:

Heather: Every Leo needs a good dose of reality from time to time and this remedy holds the key. Perfect remedy for cats who are self-involved. Custom-made for those concerned with getting round-the-clock attention from their guardians, being fed constantly, etc. This is the grounding elixir they need to give them a reality check.

Bach Flower Remedy #2:

Impatiens: Helps Leo cats tolerate other animals. Offers them understanding of, and patience with, others. Especially helpful for jealous Leo cats in situations where he must welcome new family members such as a new baby.

79

Most Popular Hangout:

On any chair that slightly resembles
a throne.

Favorite Cat Game:

Please go out to your local pet shop and purchase a synthetic bird and watch your Leo pretend that your bed is a lookout tower and your houseplant a tree. Your cat will hide and pounce on his new toy with the grace of a wildcat. Just remember not to chuckle aloud at his antics as Leo is easily embarrassed!

Favorite Day of the Week: Saturday

The first day of the weekend is the time
the house is the most likely to be filled
with admirers disguised as company.
Let the party begin - but no sticky-fingered
kids PLEASE!

Favorite Quote:

"Dogs come when they are called;
cats take a message and get back to
you later."

- Mary Bly

Virgo

24 August-23 September
THE VIRGIN

Element:
Earth

Ruler:
Mercury

Dominant Feline Virgo Traits:
Sensuousness, Shyness, Empathy

85

Profile of a Virgo Cat:

You have a smart cookie in a Virgo cat. Virgo pussycats find pleasure in serving others and realize that through giving they receive their highest reward.

Felines born under this sign make wonderful companions for the psychically challenged, blind and hearing impaired. They understand what their guardians need from them and are happy to oblige. Often referred to as the "Buddy of the Zodiac".

Purrs: Virgo cats regard lazing around in the warmth provided by a sun-streaked windowsill as sport. They take their down time very seriously and are cats in the most organic sense. This is not to say, however, that they are selfish. By no means! In fact, they will intuitively shadow their guardian if they sense that you are experiencing loneliness or fear and will stand guard at the door for you throughout the night.

Grrs: Virgo cats are very finicky about their food. They do not appreciate being fed supermarket brand cat food (only the best health food variety will do) and will react negatively to any sudden changes in their diet. They abhor houses that reek of cleaning chemicals and have been known to object to harsh smells such as incense or air fresheners.

Bach Flower Remedies for Virgo Cats #1:

Centaury: This is perfect for cats who always try to please their guardian, without consideration for themselves. Gives your Virgo cat the strength to take care of himself and his own well being.

Bach Flower Remedy #2:

Olive: Virgo's need to please can leave this cat feeling spent at the day's end. This remedy will combat feelings of exhaustion (emotional and physical) and revive mental health.

91

Most Popular Hangout:

On the windowsill watching the birds go by or standing guard behind your door playing guard cat.

Favorite Cat Game:

It is going to take some pretty serious prodding to break your Virgo pussycat out of his composed nature—so be a good guardian and get him going! Get him ready for fun by tickling his ribs, talking to him in a high pitched voice, dancing around him, etc. and you will see him turn back into the kitten he once was.

Favorite Day of the Week: Sunday

Lazy, relaxed Sunday will make for a lazy, relaxed kitty.

Favorite Quote:

"I love my cats because I love my home, and little by little they become its visible soul"

-Jean Couteau

95

Libra

23 September-22 October
THE SCALES

Element:
Air

Ruler:
Venus

Dominant Feline Libra Traits:
Pushiness, Charm, Intelligence

Profile of a Libra Cat:

A Libra kitty cherishes his family so intensely, that he is the sort of cat who will pace and cry behind your door all day until you come back from work. He will adjust himself to your schedule and expect you to come home at the same time each evening. If you happen to be late don't be surprised to find your Libra cat ignoring you—you can only blame yourself. You should know that while you were selfishly having dinner with friends, your poor Libra kitty had reverted back to his primal nature and behaved as he would if he were in the wild, mourning a member of his pride who had obviously been eaten by wolves.

A Libra guardian should pay special attention to his sensitive nature and not cause him undue worry. A Libra cat has a heart spun from pure gold and will turn even a non-cat person into an instant ally. Often referred to as the "Heart of the Zodiac".

Purrs: Eating. Boy, does this Libra kitty know how to put it away! She will eat people food, baby food, cat food, dog food, birdseed (maybe), you name it! She always seems starved and will trick anyone into thinking she hasn't been fed for days.

She also has a thing for warm laundry fresh out of the dryer. She can sleep on the comfy pile for hours—waking only to munch on crunchies.

Grrs: Libra cats can be pushy with guests. Somewhere lurking behind that sleek, cat exterior is a puppy waiting to emerge. She enjoys sniffing your company's shoes, skin, clothing and likens it to reading a good book. She hates it when she is shooed away by non-cat lovers who label her interest in them annoying.

She also dislikes loud people and especially those greedy humans who wont share their food!

Bach Flower Remedies for Libra Cats #1:

Honeysuckle: Unfortunately, in this world, everyone loses someone dear to them. It is the cycle of nature. No cat takes a loss harder than a Libra kitty. If a favorite person or companion animal has been taken away from him due to a move or death, he may stop eating, grooming and caring for himself completely. It is not uncommon for these cats to die of broken hearts. Therefore, it is crucial for their well being to offer them a Honeysuckle remedy to help them deal with any loss they may be experiencing. This remedy will teach him to love again.

Bach Flower Remedy #2:

Rescue Remedy: Absolutely all feline members of the Zodiac family can benefit from this extra special con-coction at one time or another. Rescue Remedy is a special combination of Rock Rose, Cherry Plum, Clematis, Impatiens and Star of Bethlehem. It is especially useful for emergency situations, stress and shock. Helps to calm the emotions and is useful for times when your Libra must adjust to fate's cruel hand.

Most Popular Hangout:

In your bed, on your pillow (whether or not you
are in bed).

Favorite Game: Libra cats enjoy a competitive game of tug of war with their person. While she does not have the same teeth and jaws of a dog, don't let on that you know this! Play along and pretend to strain against the strength of your Libra Wondercat!

Favorite Day of the Week: Mondays

Most people do not choose Monday to go out to dinner, which means what else? They cook in. Maybe that means there will be some extra grub for kitty to share!

Favorite Quote:

"There is no snooze button on a cat who wants breakfast"

- Unknown

Element:
Water

Ruler:
Pluto

Dominant Feline Scorpio Traits:
Strength, Intuition, Passion

Element:
Water

Ruler:
Pluto

Dominant Feline Scorpio Traits:
Strength, Intuition, Passion

Profile of a Scorpio Cat:

The Scorpion feline is a resourceful, intelligent soul who has the ability to "see right through you." Similar to Pisces, she has an innate ability to empathize with you and can read your emotions like a bonafide psychic. She will sense when you require her constant companionship and, at the same time, understand your need to be left alone.

He has a tendency to act particularly spooky on Halloween so be prepared for anything on October 31. Jumping out at you when you least expect it is a favorite pastime.

Purrs: If a Scorpio cat has been ignored for too long, she just may roll around on her back, covering her eyes with her paws because she knows just how utterly adorable she looks striking this pose. She loves to engage her human family in cat games. For example, a Scorpio cat will enjoy sitting on top of the television waving her tail playfully over the screen to get your attention.

Here is a tip, when your back is bothering you lay down on the floor before your Scorpio. She will climb on your back and walk around giving you her own brand of Shiatsu!

Grrs: Traveling. Like most members of the Feline Zodiac, traveling can be very taxing on a Scorpio cat. He hates to be confined to a cat carrier and does not feel safe being out of his element. Trips to the veterinarian are especially scary, and he will need your words of encouragement throughout the trip.

Bach Remedies for Scorpio Cats #1:

Rock Water: For those Scorpio kitties who take on the weight of the world—or at least that of their human family. Scorpio cats often feel as if everything is their fault. For example, if they are in the presence of an argument they may question their role in the fight, wondering if the cat litter they tracked through the house was the cause for so much yelling among their guardians.

Therefore, they need Rock Water to help them understand that they must not be so hard on themselves and that some things are out of their control.

Bach Flower Remedy #2:

Gorse: Helps with feelings of hopelessness and despair. Offers comfort to Scorpio cats who pick up on their person's moods and feel depressed themselves.

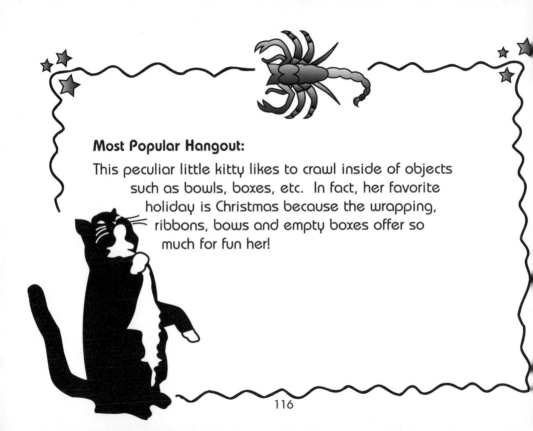

Most Popular Hangout:

This peculiar little kitty likes to crawl inside of objects such as bowls, boxes, etc. In fact, her favorite holiday is Christmas because the wrapping, ribbons, bows and empty boxes offer so much for fun her!

Favorite Game:

Scorpio kitties are born hunters so be sure to place a bell around his neck to warn unsuspecting nature dwellers. The chase is really the most fun for him anyway. He will not be content unless he has time to be in the great outdoors—so for all your city folk buy a cat leash and start walkin'!

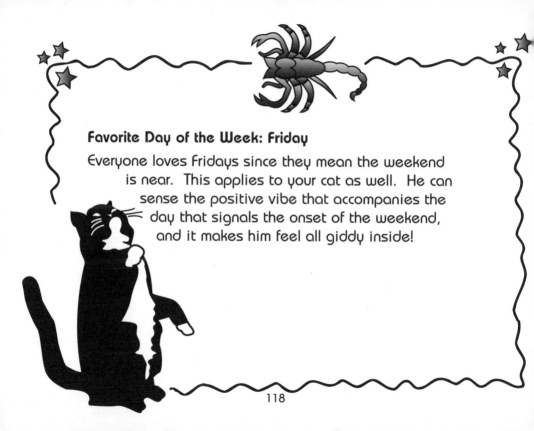

Favorite Day of the Week: Friday

Everyone loves Fridays since they mean the weekend is near. This applies to your cat as well. He can sense the positive vibe that accompanies the day that signals the onset of the weekend, and it makes him feel all giddy inside!

Favorite Quote:

No matter how much cats fight, there always
seems to be kittens."

- Abraham Lincoln

Sagitarius

22 November-21 December

THE ARCHER

Element:
Fire

Ruler:
Jupiter

Dominant Feline Sagittarius Traits:
Cheerfulness, Playfulness, Adventure

Profile of a Sagittarius Cat:

Who can resist this kitty? Everyone who crosses paths with your Sagittarius feline will beam in the presence of this playful cat. She will hold her tail high in the face of evil and find good in every aspect of life. Though cats are born hunters, don't

be surprised to see your little one innocently watching a bird or gopher go about their daily business without ever attempting to pounce on the poor, unsuspecting creature. Her heart is the purest you'll ever find.

She loves to squint her eyes at you which is, by the way, the way in which cats smile. It would make her heart sing if you would lower your eyelids to her in return!

Purrs: Caution: Sagittarius cats love to chew—and often on things that are dangerous (plastic bags, electrical wires, etc.). Always spray deadly household items with Bitter Apple (a bad tasting spray that should be used only on life threatening household objects, available at most pet supply shops) - it can save her life.

Sagittarius cats also have a thing for chewing on spools of yarn and plants so be sure to check which of yours, if any, are poisonous. When nothing else is available she may be forced to nibble on your ear while you are sleeping. Hey, it could be worse...at least someone loves you for you!

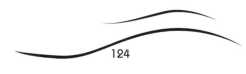

Grrs: He loathes being alone and is very unhappy being the only kitty in the house. In this world there are literally millions of strays who need loving homes, and this little guy wants you to go to your local shelter and bring one home for him (or two or three...)

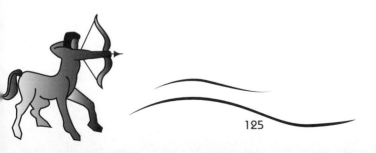

Bach Flower Remedies for Sagittarius Cats #1:

Sweet Chestnut: While Sagittarius cats are jovial by nature, they also have a tendency to experience life in a very serious way. Therefore, the occasional dose of Sweet Chestnut can help your Sagittarius cat deal with the changes that life hands him. This remedy will be an important tool in helping him cope with feelings of helplessness and anguish.

Bach Flower Remedies for Sagittarius Cat #2:

Wild Oat: This remedy will soothe your Sagittarius cat when she is feeling bored and useless. Cats, like humans, need a purpose in the world albeit being a companion, protector, etc. Wild Oat will increase your cat's ability to focus on tasks that are important to her such as "guarding" the house at night when you are away or "watching after" a small child.

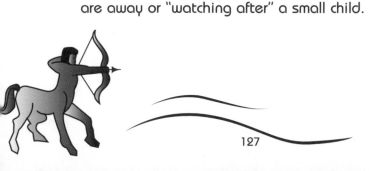

Most Popular Hangout:

Nose pressed to the window watching the world go by or spying on nature behind a big leafy shrub (for those lucky kitties with safe backyards to inhabit).

These cats also crave the feel of cold tile against their fur on sticky, hot summer afternoons.

Favorite Cat Games:

If you think for a minute that twirling a piece of ribbon in front of a Sagittarius' nose is going to make her want to play with you, think again! You will have to be more ingenious than that. Try going down to your local pet shop and purchasing some groovy catnip bubbles for her to follow, and then you'll be in business!

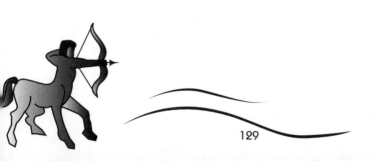

Favorite Day of the Week: Sunday

At least one member of the family is bound to be at home to keep this Sagittarius cat company and that is good enough for her.

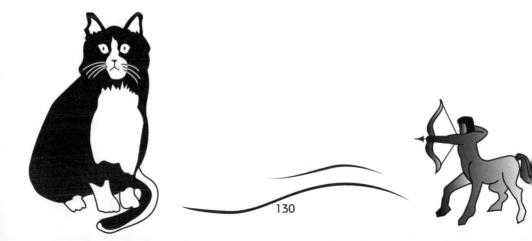

Favorite Quote:

"One cat just leads to another."

- Ernest Hemingway

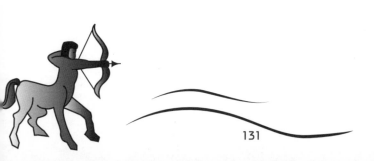

Capricorn

22 December-20 January
THE GOAT

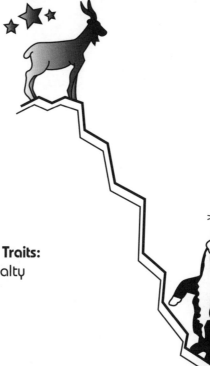

Element:
Earth

Ruler:
Saturn

Dominant Feline Capricorn Traits:
Ambition, Intelligence, Loyalty

Profile of a Capricorn Cat:

Regardless of his age, you can be sure that your Capricorn cat will be eternally regarded as the "grandfather" of the Zodiac pack. Even in kitten-hood, he is often the first to walk away from his siblings on a mission to explore the world. He also has an unpredictable side, shy one moment and aggressive the next.

Emotions run deep with these
Capricorn kitties who view all the
world's inhabitants as their "children".
Their paternal/maternal side is a
beautiful thing to see.

135

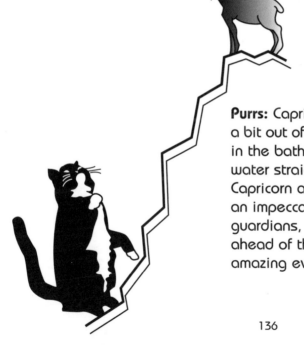

Purrs: Capricorn cats enjoy doing things a bit out of the ordinary such as sleeping in the bathtub on hot days or drinking water straight from the faucet. Capricorn also take great pleasure in an impeccably clean litter box so guardians, start scooping! They are ahead of their time and are constantly amazing even themselves.

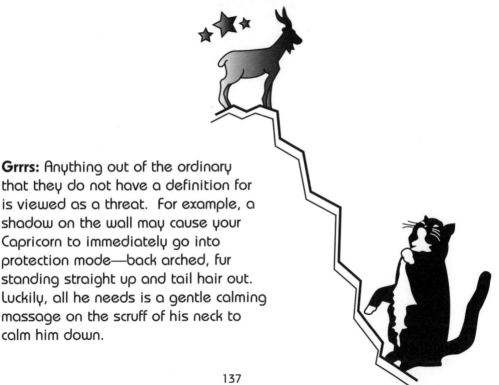

Grrrs: Anything out of the ordinary that they do not have a definition for is viewed as a threat. For example, a shadow on the wall may cause your Capricorn to immediately go into protection mode—back arched, fur standing straight up and tail hair out. Luckily, all he needs is a gentle calming massage on the scruff of his neck to calm him down.

137

Bach Flower Remedies for Capricorn Cats #1:

Scleranthus: Capricorns often feel torn between two worlds if you have other animals in your home. On one hand, they see themselves as part of the human family and take great joy in engaging in rituals such as sleeping through the night on their person's pillow. On the other hand, if he or she has siblings of the animal kind that share her home, she often feels drawn to living a nocturnal existence (playing hide and seek with them throughout the night, friendly games of run/catch/kill, etc.). All of this confusion can lead to one nutty kitty! This remedy will aid those who are often at a crossroads in their lives. It will help your cat with issues of flexibility and inner balance.

138

Bach Flower Remedy #2:

Mimulus: Poor Capricorn Kitty! So often he is scared out of his mind about things that most felines are not afraid of such as the dark, height and where his next bowl of cat food is coming from. Mimlus helps to quiet these fears.

Most Popular Hangout :

Under the bed (she feels safe there)
or tucked behind your shoes in the
in the closet.

140

Favorite Cat Game:

This Capricorn cat appreciates technology more than you can imagine! He has evolved into quite a science-savvy kitty. Looks like a trip down to the local pet store to buy a battery operated mouse is necessary for you. He will delight in watching the little mouse run around the house and will regard it as his own special pal. However, if he looks afraid of his new toy, allow him to smell it before turning on the toy's motor to assure him that it is not real, just a fun gift for him to enjoy.

**Favorite Day of the Week:
A Tie: Monday or Thursday**

These days usually involve the same
routine which makes her feel confident
and self-assured.

142

Favorite Quote:

"I have studied many philosophers
and many cats. The wisdom of cats is
infinitely superior."

- Hippolyte Taine

Aquarius

21 January-19 February
THE WATER BEARER

Element:
Air

Ruler:
Uranus

Dominant Feline Aquarius Traits:
Aloofness, Integrity, Adaptability

145

Profile of an Aquarius Cat:

Your favorite Aquarius is easily bored and loves change. She will spend hours, if allowed, to explore nature. Regardless of their sex, Aquarius cats are tomboys at heart. She loves anything that requires her to get off her cat rump and run around.

They are smart, reliable and good natured. Aquarius kitties are not eager to wear their hearts on their sleeve and will not sulk or complain unless something is truly bothering them.

Purrs: She enjoys going on walks around the neighborhood on a cat leash and can often be found balancing on top of a door intently watching the world around her. She delights in batting balls around the house and especially loves to follow the sun's rays as they dance on the walls of her home.

Grrs: While your Aquarius loves his family dearly, at heart he is a James Dean type of loner. He savors quality time with his person and hates these precious moments to be interrupted by visitors, work, etc. He especially loves butterfly kisses on the top of his furry head!

Bach Flower Remedies for Aquarius Cats #1:

Water Violet: This remedy seems to have been custom made for the Aquarius cat. Water Violet teaches the cat to release the negative aspects of his aloof nature, while retaining his independence.

Bach Flower Remedy #2:

Crab Apple: This remedy can aid in making your Aquarius cat feel more like the "King/Queen of the Jungle". Often domesticated animals are forced to hide their wild nature from their loved ones. This can make them feel depressed and misunderstood. Crab Apple can restore their feelings of self worth and make them feel closer to their primal roots. So don't be surprised if you catch your little kitty hiding under your bedcovers hunting for your toes!

Most Popular Hangout:

Look out, because this kitty likes to climb. If you lose track of your kitty, try looking up the tree in your backyard or in your attic, as chances are she can be found there curled up in a ball fast asleep.

Favorite Cat Game:

Images easily captivate little Aquarius cats so turn off the lights, break out your flashlight, shine it on the wall and use your hands to create bats, birds and the like. Your pussycat will be amazed at your ingenious talents!

Favorite Day of the Week: Saturday

Aquarius cats love to see everyone having a great time, and Saturday is usually the day people do!

Favorite Quote:

"As every cat owner knows, no one owns a cat."

-Ellen Perry

Pisces

20 February-20 March
THE FISH

Element:
Water

Ruler:
Neptune

Dominant Feline Pisces Traits:
Compassion, Psychic Ability, Creativity

Profile of a Pisces Cat:

Sensitive Pisces has the ability to see inside the souls of others. She is kind, gentle, understanding and aware. He can adjust himself to almost any situation and can often be found sitting at your feet, twirling around your legs, gazing into your eyes and "speaking" to you with an understanding cat sigh.

She will often mirror your emotions, so
please try to be positive around this kitty.

159

Purrs: When your mood is bright, Pisces will delight in every aspect of being your companion animal. She can even be found sitting beside you next to the bathtub while you bathe (soaking up that white light energy with her favorite person).

She loves soft music so when you are forced to leave her alone at home, leave the radio on for her to enjoy.

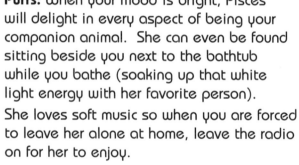

Grrs: When your mood is dark, a Pisces cat can be seen hiding under the stove. She may walk around growling at flies while hanging her head and tail low to the ground. She cannot stomach her guardians to be unhappy and can make herself psychically ill worrying about you.

Bach Flower Remedies for Pisces Cats #1:

Clematis: Helps turn a Pisces cat from a dreamer into an star! Pisces cats often sit and think about how much fun it would be to ambush their human family when they come home at night or play with their favorite guardian's long curly hair, but seldom act on these thoughts.

Clematis will send them on a new journey where they can experience life to the fullest.

Bach Flower Remedy #2:

Wild Rose: The empathetic nature of a Pisces can make her a very sullen kitty. Luckily, Wild Rose can cure all that ails her psyche. This remedy will give her back the enthusiasm for life that is often left behind in kitten-hood.

Most Popular Hangout:

Though most cats do not enjoy getting wet, this Pisces water nymph enjoys being near flowing water. You can find him in the bathroom, sleeping in the tub on hot summer days.

Favorite Cat Game:

Lovingly playing with your hair while you sleep.

Favorite Day of the Week: Monday

Enjoys the quiet after the weekend storm.

Favorite Quote:

"How we behave toward cats here below determines our status in heaven."

- Robert A. Heinlein

Other Titles By Great Quotations

201 Best Things Ever Said
The ABC's of Parenting
As a Cat Thinketh
The Best of Friends
The Birthday Astrologer
Chicken Soup & Other Yiddish Say
Cornerstones of Success
Don't Deliberate ... Litigate!
Fantastic Father, Dependable Dad
Global Wisdom
Golden Years, Golden Words
Grandma, I Love You
Growing up in Toyland
Happiness is Found Along The Way
Hollywords
Hooked on Golf
In Celebration of Women
Inspirations Compelling Food for Thought
I'm Not Over the Hill
Let's Talk Decorating
Life's Lessons
Life's Simple Pleasures
A Light Heart Lives Long
Money for Nothing, Tips for Free

Mother, I Love You
Motivating Quotes for Motivated People
Mrs. Aesop's Fables
Mrs. Murphy's Laws
Mrs. Webster's Dictionary
My Daughter, My Special Friend
Other Species
Parenting 101
Reflections
Romantic Rhapsody
The Secret Language of Men
The Secret Language of Women
Some Things Never Change
The Sports Page
Sports Widow
Stress or Sanity
Teacher is Better than Two Books
Teenage of Insanity
Thanks from the Heart
Things You'll Learn if You Live Long Enough
Wedding Wonders
Working Women's World
Interior Design for Idiots
Dear Mr. President

GREAT QUOTATIONS PUBLISHING COMPANY
1967 Quincy Court
Glendale Heights, IL 60139 - 2045
Phone (630) 582-2800
Fax (630) 582- 2813